Dennis J. Kyne, Jr

Support The Truth

Dennis Kyne received his BA from San Jose State University's school of Political Science, where he was a Dean's Scholar, Member of Phi Sigma Alpha's Political Science Honor Society and a graduate cum laude. In 1995 his award winning work, *We can transcend the existing boundaries* was published in the *San Jose Statesmen*. He has received a number of military honors and was nominated to attend the United States Military Academy at West Point in 1990. He lives in the great city of San Jose, the land of the FREE.

Visit
www.DennisKyne.com

Support The Truth

ISBN
1-59196-471-7

Visit
www.DennisKyne.com

Contents

Forward
Milan McFetridge

1.   Traitor?

2.   Paralyzed by fright

3.   War

4.   Ready for death

5.   Drill Sergeant Kyne

6.   Newsflash

7.   Support who? Are you kidding?

8.   AA take over the VA

9.   Who's the Ass?

10.   I say it is nuclear

"I spent thirty-three years in the Marines, most of my time being a high-class muscle man for big business, for Wall Street and the bankers. In short, I was a racketeer for Capitalism."

Brigadier General Smedley D. Butler

FORWARD

Sergeant Dennis Kyne, an Army medic in the 18th Airborne Corps, during Gulf War I, witnessed something he'll never forget. Bodies of soldiers melted to the hot and porous concrete. This was not the work of conventional weapons. There were no craters from the explosions to suggest these soldiers were killed by conventional warfare. Instead, flesh melted off the bone of these soldiers, as the rest of their bodies laid intact. Shadows ominously display that there's been foul play. The pictures from this mess are absolutely horrifying. Unaware at the time, the U.S. was scraping up bodies of men who had been hit by a nuclear flash! The Army was disposing of these bodies in mass graves. The international community was oblivious to the carnage. Some eight years later the country of Yugoslavia would feel the pain.

On March 24,1999 NATO began a devastating 72-day aerial campaign against the country of Yugoslavia. Massive bombs dropped from the sky, littering the Balkan landscape full of DU (Depleted Uranium) originally known as DULLRAM (Depleted Uranium Low-Level Radio Active Munitions). During this period of time, my Ujko, for Uncle, from Yugoslavia was staying with my family, here in the states. For him and the rest of my family, it was tough times. My mother had passed away from a short bout with Ovarian Cancer. Ujko was here to pay his final respects to his baby sister, the one he and all of us had adored so much. Imagine having to bury your sister then watch from an American television set, the brutal destruction of your country and people? My Ujko was torn up inside and so was I. Everyday he tried to get a flight out of America to be with his family he was denied.

Support The Truth

During the first few weeks of the air raids, it was impossible to get through to our family to see if they were alive and well. The telecommunications had all been knocked out just as in Iraq, paving the way for bankrupt giants like World Com to get seven-billion dollar contracts. As the conflict continued on, I began to look for alternative sources of news to get a different spin on the war.

In America, the major newspapers were all doing the same thing, demonizing the Serbian people and their leader, Slobodan Milosevic. They painted these horrific tales of genocide, rape, and ethnic cleansing, portraying Serbs as barbaric butchers. I knew better. So did Paul Watson of the Los Angeles Times, who was the only mainstream writer at the time with a different spin on what was happening over there. His stories took each side into account and gave voice to the voiceless. Watson's reporting was unbiased, balanced, and fair, something the mainstream media has lost touch with these days.

I continued reading stuff from alternative news agencies, and ran into some articles about the brutal and lethal weapon Depleted Uranium. This stuff was like the new drug on the block and was getting very little exposure, if none at all. I began reading articles about DU and became fascinated by the effects it was having on soldiers and civilians. I remember reading this article about a Serbian soldier who had been contaminated by DU. Within two weeks he had deteriorated into a shriveled up old man at 28, one week later he died on his front porch. More stories like this were coming up everywhere. I read accounts from U.S. soldiers who were having the exact same symptoms as the soldiers in the Balkans.

Support The Truth

I began corresponding with this Serbian Soldier, Sasha, who had fought in the Bosnian and Croatian Wars. He wanted nothing to do with the war in Kosovo. He explained to me that the United States were using dirty weapons and that many of his friends and their families were getting sick because of them. Deformed babies started surfacing just like in Iraq, where the women don't ask if their baby is a boy or girl, but ask if it is normal or not. Sasha kept emphasizing in our conversations, how his health had deteriorated, but I truly didn't understand the complexities of how he was suffering. After months of corresponding with Sasha, he disappeared, we lost contact, and I've never talked to him again. I always wondered if DU did him in.

After 30 days of relentless bombing, we were finally able to get through to my family in Belgrade and Smederjevo. Most of the power in the neighboring cities was out. Many families spent sleepless nights in tightly-packed underground bomb shelters. Talking to my cousin, I could hear loud sirens in the background, followed by explosions. The bombs were landing not more than five miles from her house. I asked her if the family was going to go to the bomb shelter? She replied, "Mickey if my family is going to die it is going to be together in our house." I sat there amazed at how they could be so calm under such stressful situations. All the while, during this chaos, Yugoslav's formed human chains on bridges that were military targets. They also held huge rally's while American Fighter Pilots dropped bombs. The resiliency of the Yugoslav people under these horrific times, was truly remarkable.

3

Support The Truth

After the bombing my Ujko returned home,
although he had to take a flight to Hungary then a bus into
Yugoslavia. This made for a long trip. My family was
worried he'd make it back ok. When home, he told us that
Yugoslavia looked like a graveyard. So many historical
buildings had been savagely bombed into charred remains.
Ujko said it was worse than when the Germans leveled
Belgrade in WWII. I was bummed for them, yet happy to
know my family was safe. I began to wonder what the
future would hold for my people. How would the youth
recover from this? Would Yugoslavia became just another
third world country? A cheap source of labor for the West
to capitalize off. It turns out, I was right on the mark. In
1984, The Reagan Administration issued US National
Security Decision Directive 133, which called for a "quiet
revolution" to overthrow the Communist governments of
Eastern Europe. By disintegrating Yugoslavia and other
neighboring countries it would force them to reintegrate
into the capitalist markets of the world. And now, this
brings us to how Dennis and I started our mission in
educating people about DU.

After the Gulf War conflict, Dennis and I kept in
contact, mostly through social gatherings. We had known
each other since childhood. Dennis and I had always been a
team. We battled my brother and his friend EB in two-on-
two tackle football and defeated them every time. In 2002,
when the Iraq War talk started up again, Dennis and I
decided to become a team again, this time speaking out
against war. Dennis had personally been through the rigors
of war. I knew about them through my family in
Yugoslavia, who lived through many wars and from my
Grandpa who was a WWII veteran.

4

One day we were at Dennis' watching TV, when the "Shrub's" rhetoric began spewing from the media filters. Instantly Dennis sensed a replay from the 1991 conflict. He started putting the pieces together and then we had our first talk about DU. I explained to him what it was and how it was affecting the soldiers in Yugoslavia. The light bulb turned on for Dennis. The radiation poisoning he had witnessed in Iraq was coming from the U.S. munitions stockpile. Although I knew about DU, I didn't realize how nasty it was because I'd never witnessed the symptoms up close like Dennis had. The insides of these soldiers bodies spilled all over the driveways of their homes. A few of these guys were Dennis' friends from the Army.

After months of research, Dennis and I came to the conclusion, that DU is just another name for low-level radioactive weaponry. The Los Alamos Document distributed by General Groves clarifies this much for us. This 1943 document, explains the effectiveness of radiation as a weapon. This document also confirms there is no way to clean it up and there is no treatment for it. So I leave you with this before you read on

.   **If there's a nuclear war no one will survive, put your ass between your legs and kiss it all goodbye! Don't you want a safe environment where children can run and play freely without having to worry about being exposed to radiological fallout? If man continues his destructive path towards the proliferation of Nuclear Weapons as a means of force, quite simply put, in a hundred years we'll all be dead!**

In loving memory of Mirjana.....

Traitor?

I wasn't supposed to be here. When my conscience actually overwhelmed my ignorance I was looking at the road less traveled; An un-paved path where deep ditches consumed me and tears flooded my hope away. My march of righteousness, unlike the roads of deception, started with the truth. Truth being the onramp to righteousness, I missed it and had been speeding down the highway to hell. This journey deposited carnage into my memory bank which had been large, heavy and ugly. I had been suckered, lied to, treated like a guinea pig, and worst of all nobody gave a rat's ass. Sadly, people who supported me while I was knocking on death's door, call me a traitor now that my actions don't line their pockets. Devastating, for a patriot such as myself, that my experiences account for nothing in the big picture, my wisdom rendered senseless and obsolete. I am a burden to an already informed populace, and I have sent shivers down the spines of citizens by asking, "Can we get a definition of support?"

I am in love with the idea of being a soldier, defending the constitution, protecting America's citizens from those both foreign and domestic whose intentions are to deny life, liberty and the pursuit of happiness. To display acts of nobility and protect suffering humans; To die with an honor that is extinct in human civilization is a wonderful calling. Having done it for fifteen years, I now know I was in love with a delusion. It was one of those horrific lessons learned, when I came full circle to the question of life: Am I here for truth and justice or just to serve the best side of the story? I found the answer in my military orders to conserve the fighting strength and ensure the health and welfare of all soldiers in my command. Support of a troop has to be strong and continuous, AA is a better model than the VA. Once a troop who needs support, always a troop who gets support. The most important time is when the fighting is over; This is when the supported troop becomes a burdening veteran that is no longer economically viable. My troops deserve better than that, your troops deserve better than that.

Four generations ago Peter Bernard Kyne fought in the war with Spain. He became a famous novelist penning books such as <u>The Go Getter</u>, the story of a crippled army veteran turned lumber salesman. As the 14th Infantry's most famous veteran, the distinguished author had been a member of `L' Company. His experiences provided the material for future stories which have their origin and basis in the gruesome facts of the 14th Infantry's service during the Philippine Insurrection.

Peter B. Kyne documented the nation's response to the returning soldiers shortly after the conflict.

I was flat broke when I set foot on Broadway

dock in San Francisco. Nobody cheered for us nor paid the least bit of attention to us. L Company as we had known it was scattered and a few days after we landed you couldn't find one of them with a search warrant.

William Patrick Kyne was born in San Francisco at Second and Clemintine Streets in 1887. Bill Kyne served voluntarily and honorably like most American men did during World War I. Through his leadership in opening Bay Meadows Racetrack Bill provided millions of dollars for charity and the war effort during WWII. A true American and patriot, Herb Phipps describes Bill Kyne best in his book, **The man who brought Horse Racing back to California**. Bill's sister Nellie, whom Bill looked after when their father passed, says the compassion for the unfortunate and down and outer stemmed from his mother's teachings and examples. Phipps records four million dollars that Bill Kyne raised for the war effort during World War II. It was Lt. Gen. John J. De Witt who provided approval for the re-opening of the tracks, with militant conditions, since all west coast racetracks were ordered shut after the war started.

Conditions
- 92 percent of the profits go to the war effort.
- Race goers not permitted to use cars or buses for transportation to the track (due to gas and tire rationing). The parking lots to be closed.
- Ten percent of all salaries to be paid in war bonds, and the same for the purses to horsemen and

jockey fees.
* Booths for sale of war bonds and stamps to be placed at the track.
* Only men over forty-five to be employed, except younger men exempt by their draft boards, and women of various ages.
* The track closed by 5:00 pm.

Here are some of the checks Bill issued:
Army Emergency Relief, $175.000
Treasure Island Army Base: $56,000
Alameda County War Effort, $82,000
San Francisco County War Effort, $60,000
Stage Door Canteens, $117,000
Livermore Veterans Hospital, $30,000
Marine Corps, $35,000
Hearst War Wounded Memorial, $51,000
Navy Hospital, Oakland, $35,000
McClellan Fund, $42,000

Bill Kyne built a plant for Mare Island Naval Hospital that put hundreds of limbs on amputees, put up the money for the swimming pool at the Log Cabin Ranch school for delinquent boys in La Honda and gave fifty thousand for completion of the music auditorium at the College of Notre Dame in Belmont, California. He received countless awards in his lifetime. The **Military Order of Purple Heart -Award of Merit,** being a favorite, he believed that our military must be strong and supported forever. Phipps honors him greatly in a book that everyone should read.

9

My grandfather, Joseph Ralph Kyne, a San Francisco Native, witnessed the atrocities of World War II on land as a Marine Master Sergeant. J.R. Kyne likened his time in service to a tour of extreme confusion. "The Japanese are kind honorable people who will fight to death for their way of life." Gramp spoke of men willing to put a plane down a sailing vessel's smoke stack, "Kamikazes," (now a favorite drink at American Bars). Gramp gave me a whole different idea of "willing to die" for ones country. "They had been training in school to attack Pearl Harbor for years, we knew that before I enlisted. We should not have done anything to the PEOPLE of Japan, let alone drop an atomic bomb.......Hawaii was not a United State, maybe our military shouldn't have been squatting in the harbor anyway? Our intelligence knew they were coming, it was a sham." When my Grandfather learned that the Navy had been testing Uranium in Hunters Point, San Francisco; he left me with one message that I will never forget, "The government used up the citizens of San Francisco in a war that was ultimately decided by an Atomic Bomb, and then they dumped toxic garbage all over the citizens of San Francisco's neighborhood."

Herbert McGuire retired as a Colonel in the Air Force in 1963, six years before I was born to his daughter. He had been a young officer when Lt General Groves first spoke of nuclear testing in 1943. Sky warrior he was, and from the sky dropped the deadliest most un-godly thing ever, an absolute crime against humanity. General Groves stated it should

10

never have gotten out of the building. "Mac," as they called my grandfather, would spend many years evading the topic of the "A" bomb. Never really talking about days in the military, we would walk around golf courses when I was ten and eleven and with conviction Mac would say that the military was good for you, it kept you busy and gave you a point of discipline. I was eleven in 1980, Mac had been out of the military almost as long as he had been in by this time. A wonderful grandfather who had served a military I would never encounter.

Uncle Michael McGuire retired as a Colonel in the army shortly after I became a non commissioned officer. During basic training I'd write him gibberish letters; he'd mail me back with Col McGuire in the return address area. Amazing how much weight a field grade officer writing to you carries. Mike was extremely decorated in Vietnam as an infantry officer and was enjoying the benefits of being an old combat vet when I visited him as a Pvt. on Fort Gordon, Georgia. He was a golfer and, like father, this son played me on those beautiful courses down in Augusta. High ranking officers like Mike have a way around the local community in the South, we walked turf I hear is sacred now. We would walk around the courses when I was 19 and talk about a different military, a more modern one. He would tell me, "If you are going to be in, there is no question, get a commission from the President, become an officer as quick as you can." I said, "Thanks, Sir, but no thanks."

On the highway of military careers, I chose the enlisted lane, the most honorable one. My second commander, Allgood, a ring knocker, gave me an active duty nomination to the United States Military Academy at West Point, I would have made General. Uncle Mike mentioned pulling a few strings to get me in to flight school where I could have been a Chief Warrant Officer. I took the physicals and was fit enough to attend both, flight school after West Point. My Christmas present of 1989, was the Panama invasion, which put all of my new dreams on hold. The following Christmas of 1990, was Desert Shield, and 1991 put me to work in Desert Storm. Allgood had vanished between holidays so we went to Desert Storm with a guy commissioned into the National Guard, and we got abused like step children. When the dust settled, I realized that the officers of our military are generally inept, incompetent and without question educated in an outdated and idealistic version of war. I became a non commissioned officer, and was on target to become a Command Sergeant Major, the highest ranking non commissioned officer in the army. Major George Arps wrote in January of 1919 in the Infantry Journal

"In a very true sense an army is constructed by its non-commissioned officers, especially the top and senior duty sergeants, who…constitute the foundation of the service…An intelligent, forceful, fighting sergeant….is one of the greatest agencies in arousing the latent dynamic fighting force hidden in every red-blooded recruit."

When I *volunteered* for drill sergeant school, the real symbol of excellence for a non commissioned officer, most of my laid back pals in California were shocked. Credited with being the best cadence caller in my graduating class, I was a true motivator and endless advocate for the troop serving the nation.

There are four central roles I play as a non-commissioned officer: commander; trainer; combat leader; ethical example. FM-22-100 (Military Leadership) the Bible of a drill sergeant, describes the duty, "to ensure that each troop is well trained, highly motivated, ready and functioning." The non commissioned officers guide tells me, "A **commander** is any leader who directs and controls soldiers as an official part of his duties." That is where my first role is fulfilled, having been entrusted with the health and welfare of thousands of young men and women serving our nation, my success shows in my soldiers ability to keep themselves alive in difficult situations.

All basic instruction of enlisted men is given by a non commissioned officer, this is my second role. The NCO handles all elements of the training, from planning and hands-on training to post action reviews. The NCOs are responsible for the army's most crucial and essential training. Many troops who enter our military do so without the basic abilities to read, write, or even speak intelligibly, this is what makes training much more imperative. In my tours of training posts I have found soldiers who hadn't the slightest idea about anything that existed outside their own world. Cleaning a weapon? Conserving supplies? Water intake? Need to be trained in eight weeks? In the eight weeks they meet swamp foot, ticks crawling in their ears, doubling up in a pup tent on the side of a hill in the snow.....sliding down the hill into the snow and waking up with minor frostbite.

"That'll teach them," Drills would say.

Just a junior NCO, I would ask, "Why didn't we teach them before they pitched the tent?"

"Shut uuuuup, fucking airborne/EFMB pussy, how did you get all that shit on your uniform?" was the response.

In Combat I have direct control over my soldiers which demands demonstrating good relations with and confidence in my own commanding officers. Faced with a platoon of soldiers who know the commands are bullshit I must not let the bullshit roll down on them. Commanders enjoyed my dedication and the ease with which I performed the orders of the day. Badges that adorned my fatigues showed I was a fearless airborne soldier, who had been awarded the coveted Expert Field Medical Badge (EFMB). "Doc Kyne," is who the smart ones yelled for when the troops started falling out. "Sergeant Kyne" is who they came to when it looked like all leadership had left the theatre. "Dennis" is what they said breathlessly after their life had been saved.

These qualities of character make my most important role a moral and living example of the military honor and traditions that date back centuries in my family. General Vuono, who served as Chief of Staff/Army for the three years I was on Fort Benning, GA says of the NCO Corps, "They are the Army's soul because they represent and demand the soldierly virtues of dedication, and discipline, and sense of responsibility...." I am the NCO that General Vuono and others seek out for advice. Who is more aware of when the ethical line has been crossed? These values Vuono speaks of are not rules and regulations to me; I have been entrusted with the health and welfare of the soldiers. Ethically I have a moral obligation as Spike Lee says to, "Do the right thing."

Had I attended West Point the moral compass would point the same direction. One of the eight major areas for emphasis in the development of these young warriors is the ability to, "recognize moral issues and apply ethical considerations in decision making." This academic instruction includes an honor code that indoctrinates teenagers into chain of command responsibilities that create their formulae for military morality. This ethical education creates a moral world for young troops long before they have even found the criteria by which to define morality. Military morality as an academic study is the finest of oxymoron's. This education is, "No one gets left behind." The true test of an officers morality does not come from who might be left back, but rather what are we doing up front in the first place?

That is not the lesson though, the lesson is this: The military defends Democracy. As troops we are taught to protect Democracy, not practice it. West Pointers, Chief Warrant Officers, nor Drill Sergeants will ever practice democracy. Democracy takes to long, you don't win wars democratically, you win them with authority, and most of the time the abuse of authority is emphasized to obtain victory.

The very fact troops protect democracy means troops protect the dissenters and protestors, it is dissenters who perform the last check on a government that sends us off to kill without motive. Imagine taking **life** and not having a reason in your heart, mind, or soul for doing it. We, my ancestors, my sisters and brothers, my friends, killed because we were told, not because we wanted to, who in their right mind supports that? Then ignores the impacts of it....................

I am not a traitor, I protect the citizens for whom the flag tolls.

II
Paralyzed by fright

There was no sun shining through the windows of the apartments where I grew up; there couldn't have been, it was all shining on top of me. I was sweating profusely, but one wouldn't know it by looking at me. As soon as the sweat exited my pores, it got sucked up by the heat of the sun. My spot, 38th, in Santa Cruz could not possibly have any sand on its coastline. All I could see for years was sand. Literally, it would have taken years to cover the amount of sand that lay before me. Days were beginning to run together, we had stopped looking at calendars. The idea of knowing what day of the week or what week of the month it was made no sense any longer. As Janis Joplin sang many years ago, "It's all the same fuckin' day man." Twelve different meal selections, three meals a day, means in four days you have covered everything you are going to eat. It all becomes the same fuckin' meal. The gritty grains of disintegrated rock that thrashed my eyes during the daily sandstorms were still at my feet. The same sun that sucked the life out of me day after day was still in the sky. I needed a change, a change of scenery, a change from these miserable elements that were wearing me down.

On the 17th of January I fought my way out to the evacuation pad for what seemed like the millionth time and it struck me that no longer were the days the same. A change had occurred; life had taken a drastic turn the night before as the hit-men of America were at war with Iraq. The President of America, Commander-in-Chief, my boss, had sent five-hundred thousand troops to liberate a country that had been overrun. The country was Kuwait, and I was one of the half million men and women standing on the front line. I no longer felt that the miserable life I had been leading for months was so bad. I was now faced with an opposition much worse than sand or sun. This new opposition was not present to make me miserable, it was present to make me nonexistent. My eyes moistened as I thought of the funerals I had attended after America returned from the Panama invasion. I cried thinking about the funerals that would be held when we left the Middle-East. I shook at the thought that people might be attending my funeral. I got to the pad with red eyes and a tired heart. As we loaded up and road out, there was a new twist in the game. Today we were not just troops, supported back home, we were American troops, and we were a target. As I stared out at the lonely desert, listening to the tanks firing down range, I wondered if I was going to be shot out of the sand. This was my first encounter with emotions that many people never experience. These emotions were ones I would deal with for countless hours in the days ahead. When the sun set, and we had survived our first day of the war; My dearest friend, Scotty, grabbed me around the neck as we headed for the rack. We shared a feeling of relief, and a bond stronger than the one between a mother and her child.

As Scotty and I sat in our bunker that night, we shared a host of thoughts with each other. The topic of how we might exit this world came around.

"You know an AK-47 round will just take whatever it hits off. Your hand, foot, whatever," Scotty explained.

"Yeh," I muttered.

"You know it won't go in your leg and come out your throat like a bullet from an M-16. They called that black death in 'Nam"

I smiled at Scotty and said, "It can take any part it wants but my head Scotty, cause that shit would hurt."

This got a smile out of Scotty. Now we were both smiling, smiling to cover the fear that stemmed from being struck in the skull by a bullet.

We continued our conversation which included all fatal possibilities such as a biological attack. The idea of a chemical attack sent shock through my body. I could remember standing in a room of tear gas with the smell so pungent it stole your breath, locked your chest up, and took away your will to move. It was painful to think of a chemical that attacked your nerves and disabled you immediately, as well as permanently. We talked about SCUD missiles, short range artillery, an aircraft dropping a bomb, and God-forbid being killed by one of our own, by friendly fire.

"Dennis, please tell my wife the true story if something happens to me. I would hate for her to be lied to."

"You know I would if it came to it, Scotty. I don't believe I am going to have to though."

I was right about not having his wife lied to about Scotty's death. We made it home intact. It was the lies that we started telling the world that broke me down.

What really happened, what really paralyzed me was three days into the ground war of Desert Storm, we stopped in our tracks, we turned around and immediately retreated from our most forward position. The ground we had covered in days was passed over in hours as we evacuated a contaminated area. This came after enduring forty-five days of air attacks in which our own battalion commanders were shooting our tankers out of the sand. It had become a complete paralysis of mental ability because we had been eating pyristigbromide tablets three times a day. The paralysis became neurosis when you started noticing senior non-commissioned officers picking their nose and eating boogers. Wow, we didn't even know what to say after a while.

Gwynne Dyer, author and narrator of the PBS National Television Series' **WAR** tells us, "Battle, the central act of warfare, is a unique event in which ordinary men willingly kill and die as though those extraordinary actions were normal and acceptable, and changing weapons and tactics have not altered those essential elements of its character." So the paralysis expands from not only why we wage war, but why do we as humans see killing and death as normal and acceptable? Voltaire would answer this inquiry with, "Those who continue to believe such absurdities will continue to commit such atrocities." This seems to be the best answer; killing and death are not acceptable, however, it is easy to understand that as long as we perceive them as such, wars will continue to occur.

1990 brought the largest U.S. military action since the Vietnam war. On the second of August, Saddam Hussein, the leader of Iraq, sent his army into Kuwait to seize control of the country. In response to this, the President of America, George Bush, deployed over half a million United States servicemen and women to the Middle East **to prevent Iraq from continuing its invasion into Saudi Arabia.** On January 17, 1991, six months after the first U.S. troops had landed in the Middle East, **the defense of Saudi Arabia was abandoned** and an assault on Iraqi soldiers and civilians in both Kuwait and Iraq was initiated. The result of this was horrible as John Keegan writes in his book **The Face of Battle**, "This was not a surgical war, it was a slaughter. History may judge high technology the winner, but human beings were certainly the victims." Thomas Winship, President of the center for Foreign Journalists, explained in April of 1991 that, "since 1980, the United States alone sent about $1.6 billion in arms and high-tech equipment to Saddam. One shipment landed in Iraq just one day before we went to war against him." Much like the casinos in Las Vegas that give you

money to get you started at the black-jack table, we
were giving Iraq the weapons to get a war started. It
seems like a reasonable conclusion could be that we
were giving Iraq the weapons to fight a war against
us that we knew we would win. As the nation rallied
around the flag, screaming and yelling at the top of
their lungs, "We support our troops," President Bush
had to have been aware we were going forward
against our own weaponry. From Bush's perspective
it seems as though this was reasonable since it would
put him in the drivers seat and enhance his chances
for continued power and re-election. Bob Woodard
arrives at the same conclusion, "The decision to go to
war is one that defines a nation, both to the world
and, perhaps more importantly, to itself. There is no
more serious business for national government, no
more accurate measure of national leadership." Eric
Hoskins, Medical Doctor and member of the Gulf
Peace Team writes, "Perhaps worst of all is the ease
with which western political institutions have been
able to convince us so readily that violence against the
violent somehow constitutes a just war." Because of
the desire for power and the perception of this
conflict as a just war, Bush jumped at the opportunity
to engage in combat. It has been said that Bush was
dealing with the issue of being seen by the world as
weak and somewhat of a push over, and so this
opportunity to display his power appealed to him.
President Bush took no time to explore diplomatic
alternatives, nor more limited forms of military
intervention, in differing configurations. Without
addressing other options it is safe to say that Bush

was responding to his critics and interested in obtaining power, thus he plunged into a policy choice without exploring the implications. In addition to the President, the people of America and the role they played during the war must be explored. It is agreed upon in the political community that public opinion carries weight in the decision making process. It is essential to understand about Desert Storm that public opinion was actually formed by the government to support the government's goals. This means that while the war was waged in the Middle East, the people in America were supporting it without the true facts. Citizens were told that the U.S. was doing the right thing when in reality innocent people were being killed and the American people were being lied to. The number of civilian casualties, the deliberate burial of dead Iraqi soldiers so that the mainstream media would never see them are images of war that America never viewed. As citizens we were told that our mission was to save Kuwait and so we voiced our support of intervention without knowing the truths of the war. We did not know that the Kuwaiti girl speaking before the U.S. Senate, about atrocious things Iraqi soldiers had done, was the Emir of Kuwait's niece, lying profusely. We did not know that the oil fields in Kuwait and Southern Iraq were set a blaze by our own forces.

People asked questions, and still do in support of our troops.

"Did you kill anyone?' was the number one

question when I returned.

"Did you blow anyone up?" number two.

"Did you get to meet George Bush?" was the third and most offensive. This guy didn't make it out of the jeep.

Because the people of the United States understood Desert Storm in the Media way, far from my way, they were willing to back an attack that was promised to be swift and, "not another Vietnam." When, it was exactly that, exactly like Vietnam. A truck load of lies.

The difference, **they got support for the troops.......**

III
War

It was only eight months since the last invasion. America had gone to Panama and ripped that place apart using young men who came home and committed suicide. These soldiers, supported by the people of course, killed themselves because they were not allowed to talk about what had happened during this invasion of a peaceful country. A number of troops were killed by friendly fire coming out of the brush without their magic tape on. Magic tape is a reflector that you band your arm with so friendly troops can recognize you when night falls. These soldiers came without it because the young platoon leader had no idea what the hell he was doing. The troops were gunned down by their own friends in the helicopter coming to pick them up. Wow, we didn't even know what to believe when the 3rd Ranger battalion started tallying suicides in the barracks and releasing these incidents as weapons cleaning accidents. It was no accident, these boys were suicidal because they were told by their commanders, "Not even to talk to a psychiatrist about the paralysis of seeing your own friends gunned down by your own friends."

It was August, 1990 now, Panama was Christmas of '89, the year of the great quake in California. This was a new decade and we needed a big war. First things first though, got to get your shots. You want to talk about guinea pigs, we were the biggest fucking guinea pigs ever. Modern day heroes, supported by our citizens, we were injected with so many vaccinations that I watched my fellow soldiers crawl onto the plane barfing and shitting themselves the entire way to Saudi Arabia. While we were battling this poison the government fed us, our equipment was sitting on ships at sea. These ships would not get to Saudi Arabia until 94 days after we did. During this time we sat in a very private place, that no journalists were allowed to go, and no troop was allowed to take a picture of. This place was called *cement city* because it was an old cement factory that had been vacated. There were absolutely no in and out privileges, so for three months we sat in each others nastiness. Thousands of us in a concentration camp where the highlight of the day was a warm Saudi soda pop, and a game of spades with the fellows. This was absolutely no different than being incarcerated. When it looked like we may never move, people started killing themselves. When the Dear John letters came, people kept killing themselves. When you got in the shower or the field latrine and got snapped by a poisonous rodent you went home. If you got pregnant you could leave, if you got caught having sex you would be court-martialed. There was no booze allowed in this country; Hill-billies stuffed grapes in the ground with sugar and yeast to make "Shine," some other geniuses tried to strain rubbing alcohol through cotton balls, thinking they were purifying and it was drinkable.

Dysentery kicked in, and the diarrhea from sand ingestion churned your insides into tapioca. We did not know whether our food supply had been contaminated or some type of biological agent had been introduced by way of sabotage. We did know that food was purchased and served that had been grown in nitrogen soil, untreated sewage. We watched soldiers stay sick because we did not have the medical supplies required to treat them, we just let them ride it out. It was all the troop ingenuity that saved us from dieing in the sand from exposure. Sun beating at 120 degrees daily seemed to be the causal link between a healthy soldier and a heat casualty. Bring with this a mass exodus of fluids by way of #2 and you have a troop that has zero hydration and a brain that is cooking like a fried egg.

Please take a deep breath right now......the war had not even started. Troops were dropping like flies from immunizations against a list of diseases and biological toxins such as anthrax and botulism. Of course immunization is the same as injection so the troops were having a hard time responding to the sand and nite sewage. I mean with Anthrax and Botulism in your body who the hell wants to eat sand and nite sewage. They did though, they ate what they were given, and they ate it when they were told to.

The manufacturing process of the Anthrax we were using was never inspected, approved or even visited by the FDA. The vaccine that was slammed into our battalion, a battalion of medical officers, doctors and countless other medically trained personnel, was licensed for prevention of coetaneous and not respiratory anthrax. Department of Defense officials admitted after continued denials that an illegal adjuvant, squalene was used instead of alum in some vaccine batches. The ability of the immune system to fight off exposure was literally broken.

Another deep breath as you hear about the troops eating what they were given, when they were told to. Troops were served PB, Pyristigbromide, a reversible bond nerve agent, three times daily seven days a week. Swallowing PB is the same as spraying gumdrops with rat poison and eating them. Troops were told these pills intended to block synapses. Nerves wouldn't be burned out if a biological or nerve agent was ingested because it would be blocked where the synapses separated the nerves. OK, I was a kid, I would believe anything. Some of these troops were from the hills though, and they didn't even know we had landed on the moon. Troops such as these ate quite a few more tablets than ordered because they figured the more the better. I was projectile vomiting from this safety pill. Having just run the entire days of dysentery, I was in no mood for projectile vomiting. I quit the pills after three days and lied the rest of the way. Troops who ate too many, well their synapses never fully re-opened.

After three months in *cement city* our vehicles arrived in shambles. They were still painted green, so we had to get to work on our auto body skills. They gave us a sprayer that looked like something a gardener uses and told us to go after the ambulances so we wouldn't be spotted out in the desert with a green ride. We got them painted, we made a mess of everything. Imagine a bunch of punks out in your neighborhood with spray painters doing whatever they damn well please and pissed off because they have the shits. We painted everything we felt like and left paint everywhere.

Then we left the cell, the concentration camp, *cement city* and headed out into general public dressed up like trees with our brown ambulances. We were as under prepared for the real desert as any army who had ever showed up in the Middle East. I was amazed at how little knowledge we had of our environment and terrain. We had NEVER trained for desert maneuvers. There was absolutely no way of knowing that where we were going was going to be more miserable than where we were leaving. Our vehicles were our liberation from *cement city*, but they drove us to the depths of hell.

Where we drove had no roads, no points of reference like the corner market or the local park. There is nothing to look at, to see, to talk about, to interact with. It is one mass of land covered by sand. We were pitching tents in quicksand, I was young, I thought the Lawrence of Arabia movies were all special effects when the fellows were swallowed in sand puddles. Vehicles and people were lost in the swallowing sand known as Wadi's, *a free flowing river in Arabia*. Free flowing it was, it took a HUMVEE and kept it turned upside down, drowning troops. After I pulled my vehicle out of a low free flowing river I stopped driving in the open road that they had said any of our vehicles could get through, they couldn't.

The vectors out in Northern Saudi were much more deadly than they had been at *cement city*. To survive where nothing else human or animal lived, you had to have some poison in you. All facilities were outside so a number of troops had a testicle or buttock bitten by an upset viper who was enjoying the diarrhea in the metal bins we used. Imagine the interruption the viper experienced when he was sprayed, upset by this the viper would strike the shooting hole. When showering we stood on packing pallets and flicked a handle that dropped water from a box. Underneath this pallet was a great place for these rodents to get some water. There was and probably had not been water in this amount in these parts ever. When troops turned the water on, the rodent, underneath the pallet cooling off, would strike the shooting hole, normally just taking out the foot or calf. I went to a handi-wipe cleanse for my body, and did not use a field latrine unless I was the first one in that morning, for the other times I would drive out to the middle of nowhere, hang off the door jam of my vehicle and drop ass.

The command decided that these vectors needed to be rid of, so they ordered in the pesticides. Root word here "pest" my ass, the stuff they brought in was meant to kill more than just pests. And when they ran out of the ones the Department of Defense shipped in, they ordered up from the local sellers. I am sure they just asked, in Arabic, "what do you all use to kill some of the most poisonous things on earth." Sure enough they coated areas the troops were moving in with these pesticides and sure enough the troops got psychotic in the face of it.

The Captain decided when we were about twelve miles from Iraq waiting for the war, to quit bathing at all. I encouraged the handi-wipe method, but he had been breathing up the pesticides they'd blown all over the place before we moved in, his brain had frozen, after all the other exposures this one did the poor guy in. Our leader was rendered useless by the troops weeks before the war had even started. All of the vaccinations, PB, dehydration, paranoia, diarrhea, had sent him into a state of shock. Guess who you gonna call, "Doc" Kyne. Expert Field Medic and Nationally Registered Medical Technician. Nuclear, Chemical and Biological School Graduate and a binder filled with letters of commendation. I was there for him, driving him around, saving him from himself. And while we pushed the convoy forward to the war, he flipped out and ordered me to halt the vehicle, jumped out and donned his protective mask, did the "Gas, Gas, Gas" gesture to the convoy and had us in Protective (MOPP) Level 4

31

before we could catch a breath. Now, you are damned near dead, your body is destroyed, and you are moving around in 120 degree heat, in a vehicle, in MOPP Level 4. There is nothing hotter than this for a human being, this is hot as hell. We drove for hours. Captain's mask had fogged up, he didn't have it sealed correctly. I knew we were alive, but he knew we were dead. I pointed out a couple of un-lucky Bedouins who happened to be hanging out in the desert that day, informed the Captain we had some live ones over yonder and we could get out of the gear before I started to lose it. He was gone, a mental mess from the heat he had us sitting in so I told him, "Fuck it Sir, court martial me, I am taking this mask off." We had a good working relationship, me and the Captain, he didn't take it personally that I knew he was sending his whole unit into a dehydrated state. We were on touchy ground though; he had lost his marbles and didn't want anyone else to know about it. I wasn't worried; the stank he carried from not bathing was enough to let everyone know.

We were heading to war in bad shape and were well supported for it back home.

IV
Ready for Death

The breath of death is the most deadly when the dead revisits in your dreams, stays much longer than the final moments you shared with them, and brings much meaner and nastier visions every year. Portraits of the faces they might have become manifest into your reality. A reminder of, or a therapy to cure, the shame evaded by a callousness that only the unknowing youth or the uncaring elder could support.

Between August and January if you hadn't committed suicide, died from some exposure, heat stroke, a poison that was there, sprayed there, injected in or ingested by you, had a vehicle topple you, or gotten deathly dysentery, you were ready for the war. What a joke that is, really with extra emphasis on where is the fucking punch line? Not one story made it to us that the dissenters had been marching in Seattle, nor San Francisco. We were told the same things America was being told. Oil Wells were being set fire by Iraqi troops and these same animals were raping and killing Kuwaiti women and children. Here come the cavalry and what a clown's costume these guys were pimping. Our 82nd and 101st Airborne were driving in on two and a half ton trucks, with heat casualties climbing daily they didn't have enough soldiers to fight. Had the 82nd battled with some of the Iran/Iraq war veterans they would

33

have come home in body bags. This was the beginning of urban training. We needed to get back home and study up on urban warfare. Had America made a run on Baghdad, the troops who were still breathing would have been slaughtered by hardened veterans. This is the first, and most independent reason we did not go to Baghdad, we were incredibly under prepared, under trained, and the incompetence of our foot troops was becoming apparent to our enemy who was pulling back into Baghdad and waiting for us. U.S. Marines our most honorable warriors took untold casualties in Kafji shortly after January 17th, the day America started dropping bombs all over Kuwait and Iraq. While pilots started shooting their own troops out of the sand, the Iraqis were knocking the Marines around. When MIT released independent research that we had a 75% friendly fire casualty rate, I concluded the other 25% were from Kafji and short range small arms conflict. Iraqi tanks didn't get a round out of the barrel, and all our tank casualties resulted from US commanders killing our enlisted troops. Here's why that happened: Flight badges are awarded to officers when they graduate from flight school. Combat flight badges are awarded to officers when they obtain combat flight hours. You can see the tension this creates........ a battalion commander has to get some combat flight time to get his combat flight badge. Battalion commander's might get a training day a year and it isn't in the deserts of the Middle East. Commanders would get up and lose their minds in the sand storms. Lacking any points of reference or terrain recognition skills, these officers flew with no knowledge as to where they were going, or which side the enemy was on. Most cried into the transmitter and started picking their own troops out of the sand while they pissed themselves in fear. There was one announced dismissal, others were promoted. These promotions are salvation and the reminder of service where troops die, and mistakes happen. While fault exists there is no blame. There is no motive therefore no guilt. No knowledge, still none, and never will be of who made money, who the troops killed for and who the troops died for.

Helicopters started getting shot down by friendly fire, it became who gets who first between the United States and itself. The grenade launchers, the tanks, the LAW rockets all got aimed at helicopters and took them out of the sky. Seemed we could have been told, "if you see a helicopter it is ours," and actually that was true, there hadn't been one Iraqi helicopter spotted. Clearly this is indicative of a ground troop who is scared shitless about the fact that officers are flying around in million dollar machines engaging them with depleted uranium munitions. More clearly, it is indicative of why they were the only ones using the airspace and killed by friendly fire. Officers driven insane by the realities of this desert were at the wheel of death. Iraqi helicopters didn't fly in sand storms, while our pilots had no problem trying to get the full eight hours a night that a chopper could fly. Longer than that and the engine would lock up from sand ingestion.

Daylight hours were spent cleaning the engines, these birds flew at night. Sand and 120 degree heat would force them out of this war if it didn't get done this way. Officers needed to go up for these eight hours, regardless of enemy activity or not, most times activity wasn't only unapparent but actually nonexistent. They went up in pursuit of the coveted combat patches, competed and won against the element of death. Sadly the element of death was our own; We brought it to the middle east with us and used it against ourselves. US troops and extreme geographical ignorance were the only barriers between a General and his "BADGE" of courage.

Pinpoint Precision Bombing is when armed forces drop bombs on warehouses filled with chemical, biological, and radioactive agents. These materials were thus blown all over the theatre while we walked around and the ARMY continues to deny that this is a problem. Many of these locations were food factories and water purifying plants, and many more were civilian homes and markets. Necessary precautions should have been taken to prevent contamination in these areas. Precautions did not exist, we literally exposed our soldiers to the contaminants by bombing and tried to accuse Saddam of using them. While the DOD keeps insisting there is no problem, top officials in the Pentagon have decided to turn their heads the other way and continue to leave civilians and soldiers exposed to these harsh conditions. Troops needed to have medical support and sites set up for immediate clean-up. It is a fact that US soldiers died from mistakes and continued to do so long after the war ended. U.S. troops violated the Geneva Conventions not only against the Iraqi people but against U.S. Troops and U.S. people.

The tanks had not even been in a battle and we were taking ground casualties, the helicopters had no confirmed enemy kills and were being picked out of the sky, we were doing such a great job of taking ourselves out we started a blitzkrieg. When I say blitzkrieg, I mean just like the ones Hitler used to run where he sent out his tankers and ran them like dogs until they dropped. Most of the time he could get weeks out of them thanks to the wonder drug Pervicen, the crystal meth of the original Third Reich. The reports told America it was an end run, like we were running into Iraq to get to Kuwait. Gabe Hudson calls it the, "Left Hook," in his book *Dear Mr. President*. Left hook nor end run is what our battalion commander said. He bellowed, "The 18th Airborne Corps was going to charge the hill and take Baghdad." We were going to take out Saddam Hussein who had raised the price of oil from 3 dollars to 21 dollars a barrel and Americans supported it because they did not want to see the prices at the gas pump go up. "Hooah," we cheered like we were getting ready for the Rose Bowl. But the Wadi's left no access to Baghdad by way of the desert . In hindsight, the fact that absolutely nothing lived any where near our locations should have spoken very intelligently to the intelligence community that we had no access. The engineers couldn't pave the roads fast enough for the vehicles that were needed to support these tankers. Engineer battalions would lay diesel fuel in the sand to build roads and airstrips. There was absolutely no way to pave roads at the rate a blitzkrieg needs to go to be a real blitzkrieg. Engineers that had been training in building bridges across rivers were now trying to figure out how to get sand and gas to turn into pavement. If there had been a camera overhead Desert Storm I am sure the viewer would have figured they were looking at a cast of mildly retarded people dressed up like trees running around like a scramble of ants who just got hosed. I went to my first Special Olympics at ten and my first Special Operations at eighteen. I feel safer and in better company with Special Olympians than I do with Special Forces.

There was no enemy, but everybody knew that right. The pictures show Prisoners of War who weren't in any shape to be awake let alone fighting. "Saddam," Lucky (POW #37832) told me, "sent us down with brand new money and told us we would be taken prisoners, be fed, get water, and be released when the war was over. I was in charge of getting the civilians down here because I had been injured in the Iran - Iraq war and this was soft duty and I knew it." If you were watching the same war I was in, this spoke very highly to not only the Iraqi militaries techniques, but also to the fact that they knew how silly we fought wars. If you watched it at home, you might have thought they were giving up. They

38

weren't. They had been paid brand new Iraqi Dinars to go to the border and be a bag of rocks for us to carry around until the war was over. This lack of understanding would prove fatal twelve years later when America re-entered Iraq with the misguided notion that they had given up years before.

Sometimes an Iraqi soldier did not speak English, and I spoke no Arabic, but we would find ourselves speaking Spanish at each other. Of course, Spain had been here years before trying to take over, and left their wonderful language for the Arab world. What my Spanish learned me was the enemy had determined that there was no sense staying in the southern borders of Iraq and in Kuwait and trying to fight thirty-four of the world's militaries. There was no Republican Guard behind them, there wasn't even a bottle of water behind them. Iraq retreated and again the United States performed one of the most inhumane acts ever in the history of combat. U.S. airplanes flown by pilots who are confirmed to have been under the influence of met amphetamines dropped uranium munitions all over Kuwait, southern Iraq and a retreating convoy of human beings both civilian and military.

Sadly the pictures showing the Highway of Death never got circulated by the mainstream media. The set of pictures showing the engineers digging ditches and bulldozers pushing this carnage down and covering it never got circulated either. The idea behind this was explained to the troops at the lowest level as, "The Iraqis will not come and clean up all this mess, they will leave their dead out to rot. We are going to do a favor and clean it up for them." Really what we were doing was hiding the bodies from the media, if the world had seen what we were looking at, they would have all turned against America. What we were looking at was a road riddled with Depleted Uranium.

While some troops were killing each other, driving into Wadi's, and falling over from exhaustion, others ran into a nuclear wall that our bombs had put up. Depleted uranium shells are used to penetrate armor, especially tanks. Desert Storm presented a ferocious war crime when the strung out pilots of the A-10 Tank buster planes rained down almost a million DU rounds. Total DU dumped on the Middle East in the winter of 1991 was three hundred tons plastered around Iraq and Kuwait. This radioactive waste that was dumped on the battlefield became the end of the Blitzkrieg. Troops walked into this contaminated area and immediately complained of illnesses that were unexplainable, without this highway being cleared of nuclear waste we had no way of getting to Baghdad. Our foot soldiers were useless, our tankers were getting shot up by the commanders. Those who didn't get shot drove into Wadi's, and the ones still riding drove into depleted uranium. That is when the cease fire arrived, one of the less retarded ones, Stormin' Norman, must have gotten tired of watching us kill ourselves.

40

V
Drill Sergeant Kyne

"Good afternoon battalion."
"Good afternoon, Drill Sergeant."
"My name is Drill Sergeant Kyne, the next
block of instruction that I am going to name, explain,
demonstrate, and you are going to conduct practical
work on is the thirty inch step from the halt. Is that
clear Privates."
"Yes Drill Sergeant."
(Said at around 250 words per minute) "The
thirty inch step from the halt is the first step you take
in marching. It is a two part command. The
preparatory command is forward, the command of
execution is march. On the preparatory command
forward of forward march you will shift the weight of
your body to the heel of your right foot. On the
command of execution march of forward march you
will step off thirty inches with your left foot. Is that
clear Privates."
"Yes Drill Sergeant."

Those who are familiar with the Stanford
Prison Experiment will recognize this is the formula
for a huge psychological problem.

If you understood the thirty inch step
paragraph reading it only once, you are a great mind
or you are a veteran. No private ever knew what that
meant, but they knew to say, *"Yes Drill Sergeant,"* or
get smoked. You can see the first lesson is actually

"Yes Drill Sergeant," not the thirty inch step from the halt. From here you get to, "Yes Sir," "Yes Ma'am," and "Roger that," or get smoked. From here you are eating pyristigbromide tablets, nite soil, sand, getting a shot in the ass and getting shot at by these same fools and saying "Yes, Yes, Yes," all the way to the grave. During Vietnam, Richard Nixon's attorney general, William Saxbe, said of Nixon's Christmas bombing of Haiphong Harbor, "He's out of his fucking mind." While Bush was bombing in Panama on Christmas of 89, all you heard was "We support the troops," and that is all that has been said since.

Yes sir, the air force is willing to drop bombs on innocent civilians and U.S. marines and soldiers. We do it proudly, in the name of Democracy.

Roger that, if we don't drop bombs there will be people alive to live in the democracy.

Yes Ma'am, taking out a shitload of soldiers and marines will keep the number of people who can talk about what really happened to a minimum.

Yes Drill Sergeant Kyne, **we believe you** can train us to survive a war.

I didn't want it to happen. An E-5, half way to Sergeant Major, Combat Airborne Medic, Winner of the Expert Field Medical Badge, who could stop me now bullshit. I had to make it happen. Having been coined at Fort Bliss, Texas for my exemplary service as a Drill Sergeant, I showed up at Fort Sill,

42

Oklahoma in the winter of 1994. I ended up under
the command of a complete donkey; without question
the true village idiot of his home town. I soon learned
that this particular company liked to kick a lot of ass.
Captain Donkey had a combat patch from Panama, no
one else had seen a firefight, a blast, a damn thing.
The way they liked to prepare troops for war was
beating the shit out of them though. I had come back
to hell. I went to Captain Donkey and told him that
young men who are serving their country with pride
and dignity do not need to be beaten like dogs as a
disciplinary measure nor a combat preparation. He
told me that I was wrong, he had seen war and he
knew that soldiers needed a beating, he emphasized
his closing with, "Now shut the fuck up Kyne." My
voicing had made me the tattle-taler of the Drills and
this became a fitting end to a career that once was
destined for the stars and the wreath of Sergeant
Major. I stayed in the military though, for fifteen
years. It took me fifteen years to realize why
everyone says, "become an officer." My entire career
had been managed controlled and dictated by these
men and women who had forgotten about duty,
honor and country and were now so mentally fucked
up they had forgotten about integrity.

While the world thinks that Drill Sergeants
beat privates up, I never once had to lay a hand on a
private. The Private / Drill Sergeant relationship is
predicated on respect, not authority. These Drill
Sergeants who had it backwards never knew that
most young officers were killed in combat by young

enlisted soldiers because the officer thought it was an authority issue, not a respect issue. If you do not respect the lips from which the orders come from, you will have a hard time fulfilling these orders. The training is about discipline, discipline does not require authority, it requires the instruction of discipline. If you can imagine the young private who didn't know that we had landed on the moon becoming a drill sergeant, you can recognize another part of the huge psychological problem that permeates the modern military. I wasn't the only Drill Sergeant that knew discipline, not authority was the desire. I don't want anyone thinking I have a halo over my head, there are a lot of wonderful men and women who believe that training soldiers is the most rewarding thing they have ever done. They are honored by the troops who have passed through their command and had successful military careers. Just like any teacher of any student should be.

"So how do you do it Drill Sergeant Kyne, How do you instill discipline without a good beating?" would be Captain Donkey's request of my intellect.
"Motivation, sir. If you motivate someone they will inherently display discipline. If you beat them, they will inherently display resentment."

As the privates ran off the bus in tight jeans, cowboy boots, the ten gallon hats, I mean big boys for privates, real big boys from the hills of MONTUCKY and the plains of TEXAHOMA, I was aware that

44

beatings were out of the question. My philosophy was if I couldn't beat the shit out of them on the streets, why would I want to pretend I could in my uniform. I stand a little under six feet and was carrying my fighting weight the whole time as a Drill Sergeant, and I watched puny little punk ass guys get together and whoop up on some young boys. I did have to get the big boys attention though. A teacher knows what it must be like to get a fellow twice your size and full of youth to stop and listen for any longer than a couple minutes. And since there could be fifteen to twenty in a company that would mop me up in the streets, I started the day they got off the bus.

After initial arrival which is where they are issued a duffle bag full of gear and a ruck sack full of uniforms, they would line up for a lesson on their new clothing. That is when I would stack their ruck on top of the duffle bag so I could climb up to the almost seven footers and look into their earlobe.

I would ask specifically, in a whisper, "How big are you?"

Private would yell, "6'6!"

I would say in a whisper, "boy don't yell, How big are you?"

Pvt. would whisper, "6'6."

"I didn't ask you how tall you were son, how big?"

" 290, Drill Sergeant."

"Not how much Private, how big are you? Real big, you know how big are you?

"I'm real big Drill Sergeant," would be the line,

because I had just said real big.

"I was going to say, I don't look like I need all
the specifics do I private, I can see you're a big boy."
"Yes Drill Sergeant."

"We ain't going to have no problems with y'all
just because you're a big boy, I mean you don't think
you can take me do you?"

"Drill Sergeant, Noooo..., Drill Sergeant. I
would never try an-thing like that"

"I'm going to keep my eye on you."
"Yes Drill Sergeant"

I found this to be a perfect setting for the eight
weeks this man and I would spend together. The
complete opposite was the smoke session young men
got because of the bigoted, ignorant, arrogant,
authoritative rules that some Drill Sergeants felt came
with the job. A Drill Sergeant is still a human, I
always wondered if de-humanizing a young man
made some feel more human. How about that for
some psychological impairment at ground level. We
as a society allow people, who are nothing but idiots
statistically, empirically, factually, qualitatively, and
from my own personal experience, to take something
basic and human which is the defense of ones family,
country, constitution, and homeland and make it
equal pain. That is the most de-humanizing
experience a nation can have.

Privates respected me, that is how you win
wars and stay alive in combat. Privates requested my
guidance and yelled for me from hospital beds and
psych wards on both Ft. Hood and Ft. Sill. Parents

entrusted their young children, some their only child, to me to teach and train to survive the rigors of combat. I will always be honored by their trust, and will have considered it a privilege to have trained some of America's finest defenders. I will always wish I knew more than I did, maybe more would still be alive.

After having lived through a horrible nightmare of a war, and realizing that this type of conduct was common in most training posts, I had no desire to continue. I had done everything I could to stay true to my countrymen and prove that the defense of our nation was my ultimate objective and my number one concern. I had been let down at every juncture and woke up to a new day that allowed me to share with everyone, without hesitation, the disgusting delusions that we had all been accepting. It is time for the world to know that the United States Military is using young soldiers for guinea pigs, not defenders of the constitution. It is time for the world to know that soldiers like me are left with few places to turn to when our conscience overwhelms us. There are few folks who can talk or even understand what it is we are trying to say about the destruction of something so pure and innocent as the young human full of hope. The young human so desirous of proving themselves, not only to themselves, but their parents, their lovers, friends, foes, doubters, enemies, countrymen and women. These young people exemplify every thing America stands for. The whole while, the people poisoned by way too much processed food have sent them into harms way time and time again for their own economic gain. Sadder is when they get to these conflicts, the officers that are responsible for the livelihood of these troops are incompetent. You add up all the experiences a soldier has from the previous chapters and you end up with a wrecking crew, not a tactical squad. You end up with friendly fire, grenades in tents, suicides. Then..............what one will realize is, you are totally fucking expendable, and even worse than that, nobody gives a rat's ass.

"Is that clear privates?"

Everyone together on this one,

"Yes, Drill Sergeant!"

VI
News Flash

Sometimes America does not win the war. Actually this is not a news flash, <u>The Pentagon Papers</u> tell us that the Vietnam war was lost the day it started, America was losing that war for a decade. Grenada and Panama, not quite wars, more like Imperialistic Invasions to take control of Central America, didn't win the U.S. anything but international enemies. Desert Storm, to be shown as *Wag The Dog*, was lost 100%. Matter of fact, America got her ass kicked.

Most folks who are even remotely conscious know the stories of our failed military missions glorified in our press as heroic acts of bravery. If one has not been introduced to the truth regarding these military operations, it is not hard to find. Searching any information stack will reveal a load of lies government has told citizenry. It might not have been made clear to a lot of people though; Not only did Americans slaughter Americans in Operation Desert Storm, not only did Americans slaughter innocent civilians and the environment, not only did Americans lie to Americans and the international community about nuclear weapons programs, Americans did lose the war. It was lost strategically, statistically, qualitatively, politically, and most of all economically. I couldn't believe the extra money spent to march us around in ticker-tape parades in

49

our tree outfits waving to the people like we had saved the world from the next holocaust. Family and friends telling me I was a hero, pals saying, "I wish I was there." In your brain rests a little known truth. Truth be told again, "we would have never made it home if we went to Baghdad." Here's why.

Saddam Hussein told Dan Rather.

"We waited in Baghdad still for them to come, and they never showed up."

Damn right we never showed up. After the urban ass whooping, the commanders realized American troops were not ready to fight urban wars. When we returned to the states, the U.S. military began intensively training for urban warfare. In a Primary Leadership Development Course (PLDC) I asked myself, "Why are we attacking cement buildings?". We were getting ready to go back to Baghdad was the answer.

Breaking News: "The United States military is the worst military. The worst trained, fed, clothed, cared for and most of all remembered for."

I have trained them, fed them, clothed them, cared for them, and remembered them. I also have lived amongst the ranks of the thirty four militaries that ran Saddam out of Kuwait. Of the thirty four, Americans were fed, clothed, cared for and remembered by superiors the worst. America came

in last and had half a million troops on the ground.
Half a million foot pounders and tankers lived like
slaves compared to the French Legionnaires, the
British Desert Rats and the Saudi Arabians who
showed up in tuxedos, minus the bow tie. Troops got
lost, shot down other nations aircraft, and showed the
average age of nineteen every chance they got. If the
means justify the ends America is a failure through
and through. America did not achieve what she said
she would. She did not foster Democracy in Iraq or
Kuwait or Saudi Arabia. She did not eradicate any
drug smuggling nor increase the quality of life and
she still has not admitted that her casualties of combat
are so high that Americans are war criminals by the
nations own standards.

Strategically the military couldn't fight in an
urban environment, no matter how mighty the M1A1
tanks were, they weren't going to be able to hold
down the city. We hadn't expected the Wadi's, so the
truckloads of airborne soldiers couldn't get through
the desert to mount an attack on Baghdad either. Of
course we had no idea the Air Force and Navy had
contaminated the battlefield with nuclear waste. This
coupled with an under nourished and un healthy
group of tired, dehydrated, poorly trained young
troops left us hopeless. We took ourselves out of the
war.

Statistics show we sustained a combat casualty
rate of over one third of the fighting force. Since the
end of Desert Storm over ten thousand veterans have

passed with 250,000 filing a claim for sickness. The
ground war had lasted three days and soldiers were
becoming deathly ill. This coupled with the extreme
lack of training left soldiers so horribly exposed to
deaths door that Stormin' Norman had to call the
fight off. Troops did not know the way around town
and had the squirts, with lungs full of pesticides,
wondering if they would get smoked by their own
people as well the enemy. That is when America
showed her average age of nineteen, that is when kids
pulled triggers like they were play station game
handles thinking the reset button brings people back
to life. Innocent people dropped dead by the bullet of
a callous young man who would later fall ill to the
shame of knowing it all meant nothing. Young troops
killed without regard. They were scared shitless,
loaded with drugs and chemicals, shitting and pissing
themselves, they were tripping the fuck out, and they
came home and learned it all meant nothing. No
matter how many parades we walked, or cheers we
heard, we knew what happened. This was no rose
bowl, this was a bunch of bullshit.

Qualitatively, the environmental destruction
that we forced upon the universe is criminal. It is
known that the oil fields were lit by U.S. troops. It is
known America dropped Depleted Uranium a
radiological element with a 4.5 billion year half life. It
is known that pesticides that were potent enough to
kill the worst of the beasts in the desert were used.
We know that Iraqi children are being born severely
deformed. We know that US soldiers are having

babies that look like the babies born to atomic survivors of Hiroshima and Nagasaki. We know that America has used nuclear waste to enhance the weapons program. We know that America is guilty of all the above and that it is in violation of the Geneva Conventions. Quality of life for all humankind was destroyed by this behavior. The United States left a fingerprint on the entire eco-system that was so greasy and infected American's should be ashamed of ever letting it get by.

Politically America ended up in the graveyard. Not only were American troops exposed to the toxic soup; Troops of the thirty four nations were sucking up the exhaust pipe of the U.S. shit making machine. When these soldiers went home, their doctors and scientists said that the United States was killing all of the allies. It shouldn't be difficult to figure out why these thirty four nations didn't show up for Gulf War II, they had taken loads of casualties last round from the allied campaign. French scientists have stated that the weapons America used appear to be so radioactive they must have come from a nuclear reactor. The Japanese started to recognize the birth defects in Iraqi and American children as nuclear. Globally it was realized America was using nuclear weapons after having agreed in 1985 to stop all of this madness. When Ronald Reagan and Mikhail Gorbachav shook hands and said, "Doveryai no Proveryai," "Trust but Verify," The deal was on, that was why the Cold War ended. Reagan made a deal to end the arms race. Reagan didn't, he expanded it and

his friends have snuck around like little fucking
weasels dropping nuclear bombs in Panama, Iraq,
Kuwait, Vieques, Puerto Rico, Bosnia, Kosovo,
Somalia and left the testing results of it in 42 states
across America.

Economically.....nobody noticed when the
economists and the political scientists started writing
about the Euro. When the European Union was being
built Americans were saying that, "it will never have
any legs." When the Euro was put into circulation
Americans were saying, "it will never be as strong as
the dollar." Well it is stronger as I write today. Euro
at a surplus, dollar at a deficit, no math needed.
Desert Storm was about the oil in Kuwait. Gulf War
two is about the oil in Iraq, but the unread war is the
euro whooping the dollar. Sirens are sounding, it is
time for America to join the world.

America needs help. The National Coalition
for Homeless Veterans stated in 1994 that
approximately 40% of homeless men are veterans,
although veterans comprise only 34% of the general
adult male population and estimates that on any
given night, 271,000 veterans are homeless.

The National Survey of Homeless Clients
(NSHAPC) study done in 1996, shows:
> 23% of homeless population are veterans
> 67% at least three years of military service
> 83% completed High School or have a GED
> 89% have Honorable Discharges

In January of 2000, The Bureau of Justice Statistics released a special report on incarcerated veterans which shows a shotgun wedding between the military industrial complex and the jail complex. 937 of every 100,000 veterans are incarcerated. 18,500 Persian Gulf War Veterans are in Prison. 60% of incarcerated vets are Army Veterans.

Among violent State prisoners, the average sentence of veterans was 50 months longer than the average of non-veterans.

Combat veterans were no more likely to be violent than other veterans.

A number that is not listed is the brig list. How many messed up troops are locked in a military jail? Nobody knows.

California candidate for Governor and former Hollywood star Gary Coleman commonly side lipped his big brother, "What you talkin' bout Willis?" every time Willis started jive talking him. My goodness, what is America doing? So busy watching reality television that they can't get enough breath to ask, "What you talkin' bout?"

Come on now, **Newsflash**: They are jive-ass talking. They are jive talking the indigenous people, the folks of different colors, different sexual orientations, different religions, different food groups. They are jive talking our international neighbors, the veterans and the citizens.

VII
Support Who? Are You Kidding?

Wondering what all the complaining is about? Or, at least my parents are still wondering what all the complaining is about. Tom Cruise helps explain it in the movie *Born on the Fourth of July*. Cruise reappears at the house with no legs, having them blown off in Vietnam, helping me realize that the preceding generation of men are always going to huff about how they had it harder. No matter whether your brain is fried or your legs are gone you don't have shit to complain about in the old tough man's eyes. Cruise's pop tells him, "You are tearing your mother up." Amazing how you are defending democracy and in a flash you are a burden to everyone around you. You are torn to shreds and people want you to sympathize with their pathetic day of shop talk. Thinking you are interested in watching reality television and discussing the days shopping events. I want to ask, "Why in the world, after having my brain stretched to the outer limits of death, would I give a damn if mom was having a bum deal?" People are inherently miserable a combat veteran quickly realizes. Unable to sympathize with a fellow human's gut pain caused by the garbage dumped down their throat has made me not only a burden, but an unsympathetic asshole. In less than six months of serving my nation honorably, I was a burden, an asshole and I had just reached drinking age. I do not think Mom's should get the bum deal though. However, Mom's are the only ones who stand by and support their shattered child. It is the Mom's who are left gluing the pieces of the child back on while all of the supporters have returned to the mall. Still gluing, sometimes years later, while the supporters are vacationing. Watching hardened glue come undone as the brain unravels so fast it breaks loose. Watching glue melt from the heat of lies perpetuated by the informed people. Sometimes not even being able to hold them together long enough to get them better. Sometimes watching them die, sometimes not seeing them before they die. I don't support this

OK. That makes sense. But, what is all the complaining about. Or at least, why is there so many people complaining? With 500,000 homeless veterans in America we have become the laughing stock of the educated world. The fact that half a million troops are out in the gutter is a disgrace to a civilized nation that continues to send people off to war. When you have carnage stacked to the ceiling of your brain, where do you go? Who ya gonna call? This carnage is so stanky, ugly, charred, mutilated that you could never duplicate it on a set in a movie room. Who ya gonna call? You cannot ask men and women to answer the nations call and leave them on the streets with no food, water or shelter. You cannot ask them to defend a constitution that does not even afford them the basic tenants guaranteed in the crotchety old document itself. How can this be supported?

Sounds good, but seriously, what is all the complaining about? Or at least, "You get medical care for the rest of your life don't you." That is what the recruiter told me, I knew different from watching Tim Robbins show up at the VA in the movie *Jacob's Ladder*, after getting bludgeoned in Vietnam by his friend who was high on army issued experimental drugs. Robbins paperwork, forwarded by the department of the army, does not indicate service in Southeast Asia. This means no treatment for service in Southeast Asia. Horrified, his war for health care begins. A war more deadly than 'Nam as his friends die asking all the wrong questions. This makes me ask supporters, "Why do you stop supporting the troops when they need you most?" I knew I needed care the day I returned. What I got instead was a stack of nonsense, 'in writing' of course. Many of my weeks wasted, "Studying the implications." Many of my days burned through with, "Come back when you have an empty stomach." Naps shattered by "Fire for effect. KABOOM." Friendships strained, friends drained, family pained. I was a burden to an already informed society. Showing up at the VA was the last thing they wanted Kyne doing. After visiting a couple of times it became clear that no matter whether you get your care on a military institution or a veterans institution, nobody gives a rat's ass. Whether it is the army medical officers or a veterans administrator doing it, they are prepared to lie about the health risks to avoid paying the people who have been injured. While the troops memory bank fills with images of death and lies, the big cheese gets his bank filled with cash. I don't support this.

Big cheese, what do you mean they get the cash and you get a brain full? Or at least, "We have known for years that war is profitable, that is why we do it. You don't want to pay two dollars a gallon for gas do you?" I am, in San Jose, California today, gas is $2.21. This is a disgrace to an already informed public. What kind of argument is you don't want to pay it, when we are paying it, and we will continue to pay it. Let's drop bombs too. Aside from the mental midget who thinks that is the issue, what about the S&L crisis that disappeared during Desert Shield. What about the Enron, Conseco, and WorldCom bankruptcies of the 2000's. Bankruptcies which vanished from the press the day war on Iraq started. Big cheese got married to big media, the offspring of another shotgun wedding that carries a sickening stench to the nostril. If a divorce is not forced, people will be reading, watching, and sharing lies. As Marshall McCluhan tells us, "too much of that television is going to have everyone walking around like drunk monkeys." While the people get sauced up on TV, the troops get sauced up on experimental juice and the money keeps moving. If you want to understand the deed, look to the motive. Big cheese is motivated by moving dollars, not euros.

You're complaining though Dennis. You shouldn't have anything to complain about. Or at least, "It can't be that bad, you made it back alive?" My heart beat, my lungs took air, my body wanted water, but I wasn't alive. Coming of drinking age with a rifle and rounds, ready to kill, ready to die, ready to get home, ready to tell the President to fuck off, what birthday could be worth getting excited about after that. Coming of drinking age in a country that does not allow booze, meant no booze, it meant coming of age meant nothing, what birthday could be worth getting excited about after that. "You made it home," what a joke. It wasn't the home we left. This home had been lied to, it had been shattered with deception and manipulation. Multiple houses were destroyed as children were abandoned and lies between lovers became deathly. Not one house in my command was left untouched by these deceitful actions. We had stayed in *cement city* like animals, lived through a horrific and deadly lie, and had come home to an even worse than imaginable state of existence.

We had cleared out our barracks for the reservists to station themselves while we were deployed. 690th Ambulance company was one of the first medical support elements in Desert Shield. It was the last medical support unit to leave the battlefield after Desert Storm. All of the gear we had left behind on Ft. Benning was ratted through by the replacement troops. As a single soldier, I moved my personal belongings out of the barracks and put them securely into a 1967 Mustang. Vehicles were parked in a military fashion, in the company motor pool, behind concertina wire, locked up behind a gate, and secured by an armed guard.

Little butter bars told us, "Don't worry about anything, your stuff is safe while you are fighting the war."

They didn't think we were coming back, we were as far forward as you could get, and folks were dead. In their mind so were we. My car was emptied and my spirit was broken. We didn't even get any support from our own damn soldiers.

I wasn't married though, thank goodness.

It was real questionable….the stories were, "His wife says she got raped." That was the explanation Ray got from his wife for ending up pregnant while he was patching up troops. Many times during the war troops were getting hardship cash advances to the family because they were told the kid was sick. The doctor bill was for an abortion though, not a runny nose. The cases of adultery were alarming to me. Not being married, I was the healthiest guy in the group after a couple days back home. We were all mentally unfit for duty after the war business. Add a wandering spouse to the equation? Murder/suicides are common after this. Being abused for an extensive period of time and returning to an even more delusional state than the one you left in combat is hysterical, and not in the funny sense. Thinking that everyone supported you day in and day out, the reality is alarming yet real clear upon return. Fellow troops did not support you, and your wife was getting stuffed in the big fluffy bed you paid for. Nobody supported us, we got used to it. I watched as troops who survived harrowing nights of combat, were crushed by the misery of abandonment in their time of mental crisis. Shell shocked. I don't support this.

Who is the silly goose saying America wins wars. There is thousands of troops who are now homicidal/suicidal and ride that teeter-totter for the rest of their life.

You complain, but, "You knew what you were getting into when you signed up. Or at least you knew they could fight over anything and you still had to go?" Huh, I thought we were obligated to the Constitution of the United States, not to the bankers and corporate clowns. I also didn't know I would spend months drinking myself to sleep at the Enlisted Men's club. Our equipment had been left in the desert so we had nothing to wake up to in the morning. We were all strung out, pictures of sugar plums prancing in our heads. I would drink all night and sleep as long as the booze would let me. When the booze war off, since there was no work to do, we sucked up tax payer money driving around collecting Desert Storm trading cards. Like fourth graders, we chased the whole set. We were heroes, with trading cards that none of us were in. We were in a constant state of identity crisis, waiting for the world to find out about us. Confused by what we had lived through and what people said they saw on TV, we did not know if we were liars or cowards, victors or famous. They told America we were heroes, we knew it was a scam. We thought everyone knew it was a scam, and ducked our heads. We didn't realize how intoxicated America was by the TV set, we didn't know how intoxicated America was by hatred. We had no idea that the support would disappear so fast you couldn't get a hand if one was free.

The debriefings said there was no need to ever open your mouth about the people being buried in the sand because Saddam wasn't going to clean up the mess we made.

The medical evaluations stated there was nothing to worry about, no illnesses to speak of, and troops were doing good.

The media, all done prostituting with big cheese, jumped in bed with the government. This didn't end in a shotgun wedding, this was a fuck frenzy that sold out millions of people and put a drain on the morale of the military and is forcing America to play the same hand Rome did many years ago. If you are forced to hire out your military, as Rome did, and as America did in Gulf War II your military will crumble. Gulf War II witnessed the largest call up ever of reserve components, and you can be sure it has had a horrific impact on the families of these troops. Weekend warriors and un naturalized citizens made up the fighting force. Soldier citizens and un naturalized citizens activated as troops in a time of crisis is who you support.
Are you kidding?

VIII
AA Take Over the VA

Step 1: Provide medical care to all the troops, just like the recruiter told us.

In a country that doesn't provide citizens basic medical care, veterans start off second in line. Everyone knows the recruiters lie. Everyone knows war sucks, being a troop sucks, sucking up to others who are sucking up to others who are sucking up.........all the way up the pole. It all sucks, but the recruiter promised we would get medical treatment if we got messed up. There are half a million homeless troops who can't get a meal, a medical exam or a bath.

"They wouldn't do that to you guys, they could never let that happen," my closest relatives say.

"It is happening." I repeat.
"Well if it is, somebody has to do something about it. They can't do that to you guys."

Who they are you talking about? The same they that is jive-ass talking the world?

I have been looking around for a decade for somebody to do something. They don't seem to be willing to step forward. If you know somebody please tell them they are being silly if they cannot keep up with the carnage they create on our soil. One half million homeless vets and no medical care, and people are still yelling, "we won, we support the troops." This is not stupid, this is fucking delusional.

In the summer of 1991 I arrived at the veterans administration to find that my documentation, like that of Tim Robbins, had no indication of my service in Southwest Asia. No indication means no medical care for service in Southwest Asia. My nightmare began as I now had to prove I fought in a lie. While other troops died in their homes after being denied medical care by the VA, I fought on. These troops would not live long enough to ever be tested, they would not live long enough to tell their story, they would not live long enough to realize it was their own people who exposed them to the death they had experienced. Chalked up to pre-existing conditions, smoking, and on the list went, they would never be recognized as casualties of combat, recipients of the Purple Heart. While the military kept sending out time sucking documents that kept medical people dis-informed about where and what and how and who was at risk, I buried my fellow troops. While I wondered if I was a dead man walking, an angelic friend Holly would remind me of our school mates name seconds before I shook their hand. While I worked myself to sleep in the middle of the afternoon, supporters were at the mall. While the civilized people of America moved on to the next current topic, troops begged for the link between life and death. A link denied to them by the same people who promised never ending support. While this was all happening, I mailed them the correct copy of my documents which stated my combat exposure very clearly.

They denied my claim. Of course they did, every insurance company does. During this period of denial, a lot die. Some seek private care, some don't. Some suck it up and drive on, some burden the public and private sector with illnesses. How can you tell troops to fight for a nation that does not guarantee them basic medical care? A Senate Hearing in 2002 confirms that "total per capital expenditures for veteran mental health has declined by 20.6% since 1995. Between 1995 and 2001, the number of veterans in need of mental health service has increased 26%." 1995 was also the year that the US government approved a payment, "a buyoff," to veterans for undiagnosed illnesses. The old, "give 'em a couple bucks and they will shut up," version of reality. Then the government stopped taking new enrollments at the VA institutions, pulling 80 million dollars from the VA budget to fight war and abandoned millions of veterans who had been promised lifetime healthcare by the recruiter. In the same breath they were creating a whole new generation of veterans who would become burdensome assholes. What kind of logic is being applied here. Burn the current crop, create a new crop, abandon them all because they are tainted crop. Who is supporting this?

I sent in the letter and the pictures showing I had walked all over Iraq and the airfield that got

66

pounded by DU rounds.

The letter was reviewed and denied, and was continually denied while they studied the implications. Results didn't say anything, and didn't mean anything. I decided that my health was in my own hands, like the thousands of troops I had patched up before, "Doc" Kyne became his own patient, and lived.

In 1995, I was tested for ionizing radiation and "undiagnosed illnesses" stirred up some excitement as the VA awarded compensation for illnesses that could not be diagnosed. What is this type of verbiage? Is this medical, scientific, philosophical or make believe. How do you get a way with undiagnosed illnesses as a diagnosis for compensation? Gulf War Syndrome, was the response. Sounds scientific enough to mean nothing. So now folks ask, "What is Gulf War Syndrome?" If it looks like they can handle the truth I say, "Gulf War Syndrome defines **nothing**, GWS is nothing but an acronym for **nothing**. It is the worst joke in an already horrible act."

Then you get asked, "do you have Gulf war syndrome?"

"No, I don't have **nothing**, I have something, but what I have is undiagnosed."

"Is that what Gulf War Syndrome is?"

"Gulf War Syndrome is nothing, at all, whatsoever, a joke."

"Well it can't be nothing or they wouldn't

write about it."

"OK, troops are ill, they can't diagnose the illness. They call this Gulf War Syndrome."

"Oh, I get it, that makes sense. Sounds like Downs Syndrome, we don't really know what is wrong with them either."

Another genius supporting the troops. This is a premium example that has been repeated to me, in many forms, of a slightly retarded person explaining how informed they are about retardation.

What is wrong?

Veterans Affairs is being run like a hamburger stand that gets washed down at night with a dirty pair of socks. It's infected with mad cow's disease, and no matter how many wonderful people put their hearts and souls into it, some asshole like Ronald Reagan takes all the money to pump his war machine and than comes down with Alzheimer's so he never has to explain leaving half a million heroes dumpster diving for dinner. First step is to admit there is a problem. Since that is crystal clear it seems to me that the Alcoholics Anonymous program is the best way to repair a troop. The Department of Defense and the Veterans Affairs are loaded up with tough guy syndrome. Administrators with six digit incomes are telling troops, who at most made six or seven hundred dollars a month, they are just complaining, looking for free lunch.

Support The Truth

A quick look at the VA system indicates that veterans are viewed as indigent and worthless by a large segment of America. A quick look at the AA system indicates that the survivors of this battle with booze are heroes, lauded by their families and friends. There are stores dedicated to shopping for them on their special days of sobriety. I like that, I support that. I want that for my troops. Doesn't America want that for her troops. An even deeper look paints a place of despair with the VA hospital knocked to rubble. Comparatively, the AA is welcome everywhere. There are meetings every day, in every city, sometimes multiple times during the day. If you are struggling with the drink you have a list of people to call, a host of friends who will have you over, you have allies in your battle with the bottle. AA has twelve steps, you know where you start, you know where you end, and you know if one has recovered. VA has no steps, you start at the back of the line, you end up at the back of the line, and the statistics are very articulate about the fact that close to nobody ever recovers. With all of the dependencies, addictions, lying, cheating, stealing and horrific crimes against women and children, America has forgotten that troops need to recover just like any survivor of a tragic event. America got tough guy syndrome from the shitty commercials portraying the military as a challenge, and although the troops are tough, they get sick, go crazy, and need to be given a road to recovery just as any other battling addict or person who is post trauma due to a violent crime, rape or beating.

A sorrowing thought is that war is profitable for a lot of people, just like alcohol sales are profitable. Like booze, America isn't interested in prohibiting war either. Obviously America is willing to have dry drunks in high places and suffer the impacts of domestic issues such as child and spousal beatings. Amazingly enough AA put together a program that if the individual commits to, works at, shows up, and keeps a focused point of discipline they will win the battle over the drink. I love that, I am a Drill Sergeant. This is exactly what we ask our troops to do. Commit, work, show up, stay focused and be disciplined. Troops respond remarkably well to this process, for that matter all humans respond well to this process. If it means admitting, (step 1), that the VA is being washed down at night with stinky socks than we must do it. That is supporting the troops. If it means handing over the VA to somebody like myself who actually knows what is going on, than it has to be done. As the Indians say, "Strong Hearts to the Front." I am hear, at the front, calling out anybody who thinks I am wrong. There is absolutely no excuse for America to have half of a million troops sleeping curbside, eating scraps from garbage piles, shitting and pissing themselves and eventually dying alone, in the waste piles of the greedy shit bags who are sucking up everything in sight.

Desert Storm veterans get a newsletter every month telling us about the new stuff that the VA is working on. I have been getting this newsletter, *The*

Gulf War Review, for a decade. It is a joke, not quite as hysterical as GWS, but it is full of nonsense. It covers nothing and restates itself month after month about the same issues they have already found to have nothing on. It is like a therapy group newsletter that is supposed to make us feel like somebody is looking out for us. Somebody is getting paid to send me a newsletter covering nothing. Ten years the VA has undiagnosed me and sent a newsletter that is without question a waste of money. In the same period I have met, talked with and befriended, many souls who have been drunk, addicted and on the skids. A great number of these people, some with Doc Kyne's help, kicked the habit and fought for mental freedom. There is a spirit the human being has that helps us stay alive, reptilian if you will. It is the basis of my original work *We can transcend the existing boundaries*. We know when we are damn near dead, and we know there is something we can do about it. Last Verse, same as the first.

"They wouldn't do that to you guys, they could never let that happen."

"It is happening."

AA take over the VA!

IX
Who's the ass?

My father, a paid poker player, often advised, "There is always one ass at the card table, and if you can't tell who it is, it is you." Who is the ass when it comes to the military industrial complex? It is the soldiers. If the soldiers are ass, this makes the citizenry worthless. You can't tell me a machine that promotes racism, gender preference, and class separation can protect a citizenry that is supposed to enjoy freedom from these discriminations. While the Air Force academy continues to treat females as second class cadets, and the Navy continues to behave in a patriarchal, bigoted fashion, the citizen actually believes they are being protected from these social viruses.

O.K. I grew up in California where racism, or as some southern politicians like to say, "segregation," isn't cool. Actually, I am from northern California, I have a lot of loving relationships with other men. I am not homosexual, but I sure as hell don't think being queer is a moral crime. Somebody explain to me this God they are talking to who is busy worrying about what billions of people are doing with their genitals.

More specifically, I am from San Jose, where Tommy Smith and John Carlos graduated my alma mater, San Jose State University. These men raised

their black gloved fists in the air, at the 1968
Olympics, telling the world that racism was running
rampant in America. They were college students
representing America and were being called
"Niggers" by Americans. These men brought home a
gold and bronze medal to represent athletic
superiority in the United States. These champions left
a nation that posted signs reading, "No colored
allowed," and returned to a country that shunned
them for, "not knowing their place." What a fucking
disgrace.

Even more specifically I grew up in a two
bedroom apartment with my father, Dennis Sr. in the
1970's. Single dads were not cool, and apartments
were just starting to reflect the real decay of
urbanization. I was the only white kid in these
apartments, and I was the only kid in my class who
lived in an apartment. Not being raised anywhere
close to pacifism I threw a lot of punches at the
schoolyard. In the apartment yard the Latino kids
batted me around like a piñata and if it was, "Smear
the Queer," I was always the first one smeared. Kids
would spit those nasty hawkers you dig up from your
lung in my face and smash me in my head with wrist
rocket, sling shot, balls. At school, where I was called
the apartment kid, I wore a t-shirt every day and
when it was cold I wore an over t-shirt. The peanut
butter on crackers and an apple I took to school
couldn't match up to all the chocolate bars and teeth
shattering lollipops the other kids were nibbling.
Heckled all the way to the trash, I tossed my bag in

the bin and hid on the toilet during lunch hour because we couldn't afford a candy bar.

I hit double digits, the 80's arrived, my father got married and we moved no more than a mile, door to door, into a neighborhood. "Movin' on up," but we weren't even close. Step-parents were still something you had to explain to people, and tract homes were just starting to reflect the real decay of sub-urbanization. Railroad tracks separated our new digs from both Saratoga and Los Gatos, where money grows on trees. Door to door a mile, opposite of the apartments, was the fanciest tennis club in California. I had lunch once on the "deck" at the club and realized quickly what, "wrong side of the tracks," meant. The kids on the other side had a pair of 501's for everyday of the week; I had one pair I wore every day because the bell bottom corduroy pants I had been using back in the apartments were not cutting it. Luckily I made a friend, my best child hood chum, Duncan who lived with his mother and grandmother in the same neighborhood. He was poor too, so at the junior high Duncan and I sold bubble gum and jaw breaker candy to the rich kids right out of our locker. We opened our own bank account and ate Church's chicken everyday until we got robbed by a rich kid who looked over my shoulder to get the locker combination. When the rich boys mother found the candy in his room she called the Dean. Duncan and I got suspended from school for five days. Now, the rich kid didn't get in trouble, nobody called the police for him robbing our stuff. What

74

happened? They punished the poor kids trying to
get up a couple dollars the American way because we
were cutting into the school snack shack's money.
What a joke for an eighth grader to hear. Luckily
Duncan's mom knew the deal, she smiled and told us,
"you have a week to find another product." So we
sent his younger brother, Milan, hustling expired
raffle tickets to keep us in video games and soda pop.

Mike, who belonged to the tennis club, lived
on the other side of the tracks and played on the little
league team with Duncan and I, came to the house
one day asking, "Where is your swimming pool?"

I said, "we don't have one."
"Where is your computer?
I repeated, "We don't have one."
"Where is your work out room?" .
I repeated, "We don't have one."
"Where is the videogame?"
I repeated, "We don't have one."
And than we both had to get on a toilet.
"Where is your other bathroom?
I repeated, "We don't have one."
Mike's conclusion, "Man you guys are poor."
My conclusion; I was *still* spoor.

I could not imagine what Mike would call
where I had been living. Inside a couple mile radius I
experienced two tiers of the class struggle, leaving me
believing I was poor.

Landing on Ft. Benning, the summer of 1988, I was shocked to realize I was not any where near poor. My shock was coupled with awe as I viewed far more confederate flags than American flags. Shock and awe, don't tell me these are Americans. Hatred, racism, homophobia and paranoia permeate the air like a thick, nasty, stinky, toxic dump site on this place. Fools down around this area try to tell me that the Civil War was about state rights, and that being from California I have no idea what state rights are. Fuck a state right or a federal right, we all have inalienable rights. I would tell these fellow troops of mine that we were obligated to defend the inalienable rights of all people. Most of them, not some of them, disagreed. Through my tours of the south I found it to be incredibly impoverished, and actually abusive to the people who want to discuss the poverty. I met folks who lived in homes with no running water or electricity. What kind of shit is this? The richest nation in the world? The most democratic and equal and concerned for the little guy? This is third world shit, that is what kind of shit this is. This is not coffee we are whiffing. This is the ass of corporate greed and corporate waste that is locking people down in the land of the free. This is a citizen being treated like shit.

Said he was white bread
Looked like he'd been corn fed
Couldn't make a word he said
For sure he was inbred

I penned this short work after a few months of looking at fellows who did not have the slightest idea they were bigots. All men are created equal is not something that all the troops believe. Many troops come from social systems that encourage beatings, lynching, murders, and verbal abuse to children, women, homosexuals and people of differing color. This system perpetuates racist and discriminating social behavior and instills a sense of fear in people when they should be instilled with honor. We are talking about people who walk in fear of being physically, sexually and verbally abused by individuals who do not have any accountability. We end up with a corn fed, inbred, white kid who speaks like an illiterate Neanderthal telling us about how much he hates, "faggots and niggers." Seriously, this is no joke.

For example:
Watkins, a white fool from Texas, gets paired up with me for a game of Spades one night while we were detailed to the Officer Candidate School. Franklin B and Scotty are the opponents. Scotty and I normally teamed up, and couldn't be beat. Not on this round though, Watkins is a racist and wouldn't team up with black people. It was late, dark, and quiet outside. Jokes started, and Watkins lets out, "what's the difference between a dead dog and a dead nigger in the middle of the road?' I look around in bewilderment, I am eighteen now, I had done it all and thought I had seen it all. Scotty, looked down and shook his head, and Watkins said, "there is skid

77

marks in front of the dog." Like I said, I wasn't raised a pacifist, I thought I was going to see this ambulance tip sideways with a black man choking a white man to death, and honestly I would have sat and watched. What happened though was even more appalling, Franklin B. assumed he was in a cab with three whiteys so he didn't let off a knuckle sandwich on Watkins's lip. Tension was bubbling though and just as I was in the middle of saying, "kick his fucking ass," the back of our ambulance was being beaten on by a candidate. This young man had used a rolled up piece of paper as an earplug while on the firing range and it had dropped down into his earlobe. Yes, this man was preparing to lead troops in combat, using paper as ear plug. There was no way we were letting this guy into the ambulance to look down his ear. I told him, "Candidate, there is nothing we can do for you. You should not be putting paper down your ear. Tell the other candidates if they need earplugs to see us before you go, we have them for you, we told you we have them for you." Scotty, who had the rank, told Watkins to cough up an apology and get the fuck out of his face. Strangled by stupidity and bigotry, I laid awake all night wondering why I had grown up believing that because all people were created equal, they were treated equal. Man I had been lied to.

Now I come full circle to the question asked initially in this chapter, what does this type of ignorance make the citizenry? Truth is that even the Olympics haven't changed a damn thing in four decades. Michael Franti **(Spearhead, the album**

Home, 1994) sings it like it is when they let the NBA
into the Olympics:

> **Fans were waving the red white and blue**
> **It seemed strange to me / was it strange to you?**
> **Brothers on the street and everyone is scared of ya**
> **So how could ten Africans represent America**
> **Bullshit, It didn't mean a thing**
> **'cause in the same year we saw Rodney King**

A decade after this, in Oakland, my brothers
and sisters are being shot in the head by officers in
uniform for taking up places of protest in the streets.
My fellow Americans are being herded around like
chattel rather than people. America has entered into
a state of martial law. No longer are the troops
defending the constitution, they are defending the
right of the police to pummel the citizenry in the
name of business. This is the most extreme irony of
all. Or possibly the greatest tragedy ever. American
taxpayers are covering the cost of there own beatings.
The United States Supreme Court states that, "The
expression of the individual is more important than
the whole of the community." Thomas Jefferson
stated that, "Our liberty depends on the freedom of
expression." Yet, our troops defend the incarceration
and enslavement of millions of Americans at home. If
the very idea of the military is to defend the
individual, by the very fact that a citizen has been
touched without permission by a police officer is a
principle upon which that police officer should be
prosecuted for violating the public trust. Absolutely,

prosecuted, there is no place in a Democracy for the over assumption and the abuse of authority. Police units are inherently an extension of the military. Using the same command structures, salutations and rank references, they now are marching around in jungle fatigues as they attack citizens and city buildings. I was always under the impression the police existed to get citizens from point A to point B safely. Why the fuck are they dressing up like trees and shooting at us instead? Cause citizens, the highest office holders in America, ain't shit.

Jefferson and the other founding fathers, the framers of our constitution, would never imagine the military turning on the citizens. Built to serve and protect, this machine actually exacerbates the very ills it was intended to eradicate. What a shame.

X
I say it is Nuclear

There is currently strong evidence to support the idea that the human species is no longer evolving. Humans, or at least Americans, are devolving into a state of toxicity where they don't even recognize the implications of the waste they create. What ever happened to, "you are what you eat?" What ever happened to, "don't shit in your own back yard?" What ever happened to pick up your neighbors yard after you and the dog drop ass all over the lawn? When did evolution turn humans into cheese-burgers, moistened with grease and soda pop, defecating over home soil and all over the world? This is advanced thinking in a civilized nation with evolved societal values? I don't think so.

My claim is this: Depleted Uranium is a Nuclear Weapon

Depleted Uranium is defined in the Government Training Aid GTA 3-4-1A, published by Headquarters, Department of the Army, July of 1999 as, "*slightly* radioactive."

I grant *slightly*, imagine having your head stuffed into the microwave and set on *slightly* twenty four hours, seven days a week, the rest of your life. It has been turned on and set to *slightly* forever. Milan cleared this up for me by explaining that with a 4.5

billion year half life, his family will be stuffed inside the *slightly* radioactive microwave for ten times that long.

Former United States Attorney General Ramsey Clark defines a nuclear weapon as, "killing all forms of life while keeping property intact." The pictures on the upper back cover meet this definition.

If the world values life itself, nothing more required, just a value of living things, it is imperative to understand that this is a weapon of extinction. Stop radiating people, the planet and the water. It appears that the impact of this uranium is omnicidal, humans are not resilient to radioactivity, maybe they should consider doing something about it.

"So where's the real evidence?" the donkey would ask of my intellect.
"If I show it to you, will you believe me?" I say over and over.
"Maybe."

Maybe, what the fuck maybe. What do these people believe through that foggy haze of nicotine and vicodines washed back with a couple pulls of hot or cold caffeine. Trying to swallow truth through a 1-800 number advertising pizza. Calling it reality TV from a box that was declared by the Supreme Court to be for entertainment only.

I don't have any TV evidence. They made us
feel large and in charge on a Sunday night at 10 pm
when they got DU on the reality box. Colonel Daxon
addressed the issue, telling the world that DU is
harmless because the human being has been exposed
to higher levels of __natural__ uranium. This Colonel is a
medical officer not a munitions expert, not a nuclear
scientist. If the army manual states it is slightly
radioactive, what is he saying? "People have been
exposed to higher levels of radioactivity and that
makes radioactivity ok." And of course I will grant
the use of the word *higher.* Imagine Hiroshima being
a *higher* level of radioactivity than Baghdad. Where
is the threshold though, at what point is someone
sucking up to much nuclear fall out? New terms
indicate uranium has been depleted to a *slightly*
lower level of radioactivity, sounds like the new
definition of a low level, low yield nuclear bomb.
Guess what? America is recognized in the Guinness
Book of World Records as possessing the smallest
nuclear weapon.

*"The W54 fission bomb, deployed by the USA
in Europe between 1961 and 1971, is the smallest
confirmed nuclear weapon ever made. The bomb had
a range of 2.49 miles (4km) and weighed 76 lb (34.47).
Its widest diameter was just 11 in (27cm)."*

This is the book of world records folks, this is
on every persons coffee table at least once in their life.
This is not new. Nuke your food, nuke your foe, nuke
your friend. It is all *higher* levels depleted to *slightly*

lower levels. That is how we got low level nukes as the newest headline. America has been deploying these things for decades.

Jim Stueve, of the Army Public Affairs Office, was sent a list of questions concerning DU with Question eight reading: Army Regulation 40-5 says: "All actual or alleged overexposures to ionizing radiation will be investigated and reported under AR 40-14 and AR 385-40. How many such incidents were investigated and reported during the Gulf War and after?

The answer came from Colonel Cherry, army radiation safety officer. Cherry writes, "Overexposure" is not applicable to the deployed army. However, even if it were, only those soldiers with DU fragments in their bodies resulting from friendly fire have the potential for exceeding maximum permissible limits for DU in the body.

Overexposure is not applicable.
WHO LET THE DOGS OUT, OR IN?

Please recall, MIT did that study with 75% of casualties being friendly fire. Wow Cherry, that means three fourths of the casualties have potential for exceeding limits. Guess who established Protocol for monitoring gulf war veterans with DU fragments. You guessed it, Daxon, who had not been promoted to Colonel yet. That senior level support was displayed when he got promoted and troops got the pokey. If Cherry and Daxon were in my moms class of 5 -7 year old Down Syndrome students, they would fit in just fine. I mean it seriously, the critical thinking level is obviously very close, looking like the students might have the edge.

Let's see if we can follow this. It is *slightly* radioactive. People have been exposed to *higher* levels of it, but even if a soldier runs into a higher level, overexposure is not applicable. Sounds like Gulf War Syndrome brought on by undiagnosed illnesses to me.

Colonel Naughton of the U.S. Army Material Command told BBC that complaints about DU, "had no medical basis." Now we have all the Colonels, one rank below Generals, giving us what my pals call the goose chase.

The medical officer, Daxon, claims he understands radioactive isotopes and radiation levels. I am calling bullshit. The radiation officer, Cherry, claims exposure is limited and overexposure doesn't exist. That is bullshit. The materials officer, Naughton, claims it has no medical basis. A lie.

There must be a level of harm Daxon understands, that has medical basis Naughton is not familiar with, which matters because Cherry says overexposure is actually possible.

My friend, Major Doug Rokke, a fellow medic

and senior non commissioned officer for nineteen years before being commissioned by the President of America, was appointed by name to research, investigate and report on the implications of DU use in the Gulf. He confirms that the Pentagon lies about DU dangers and is criminally negligent for neglecting medical attention needed by DU contaminated Vets. Major Rokke has served this nation in combat more than once in a career spanning three decades. Major Rokke now resides where he is from and works as a substitute teacher. Support the Truth, lose your position and go broke. The rest of them all made Colonel. Rokke was given a direct order to research this weaponry with the health and welfare of the troops, the civilians and the world in mind. He told the truth and got the pokey.

Manuals state the Health Risks Associated with DU for the troops as,

"Like lead and other heavy metals, internalizing large amounts of uranium could affect your health. The primary organ affected is the kidney."

Like lead? What? Lead has been banned from paint because the kids eat it up, and from gas because it ends up all over the roads and in our water runoff. Lead is *out-lawed* in America. My fucking lord, how can you use it as a health comparison?

This is the good news. The bad news is that

Depleted Uranium isn't just for the troops. It is for
everybody, for ever. Dr. Asaf Durakovic, a United
States Army Colonel, tells it like it is. "DU is still very
radiotoxic and is highly pyrogenic when ignited,
which happens when artillery shells are fired. The
intense, searing flame caused by ignition of the
uranium not only aids in penetration of tank armor,
but also liberates the uranium into the environment
making it available for internal contamination via
inhalation and ingestion." Colonel Durakovic
outranks these other clowns in the United States
Army, and is a far more competent scientist. He got
the pokey. Helen Caldicott has confirmed that the
dust-laden winds of DU-contaminated war zones
"will remain effectively radioactive for the rest of
time." Left in the ground it will reside permanently
to become a part of the food chain. The water will
have some to drink. The plants and vegetables will
have some to eat. The livestock will be as radioactive
as the people.

I met Leuren Moret, a whistleblower from
Lawrence Livermore lab, and the bad news got worse.
It took all of five minutes for me to connect the dots
between our nuclear waste of the eighties and our
bombs of the nineties. In Hunters Point, California, a
predominantly black community, there are breast
cancer rates that cannot be duplicated anywhere in
the world. The causal relationship goes to Uranium
testing done at the naval ship yard. They left DU in
the bay that Otis Redding talked about sitting in and
have been steadily destroying the black community

which was left with this atomic waste.

The Navy, what the fuck is the Navy doing testing Nuclear weapons anyways? The Navy is testing nuclear weapons now, because in 1943 United States Army General Groves working with a very capable group of scientists told the world that this weapon was in no way shape or form to be anywhere near ground troops. The Groves documentation clearly outlines one thing, there is no medical treatment for this and the impacts to the environment are irreparable. So, "go navy," drop DU rounds all over soldiers, marines and civilians, because the Navy says it is OK. My mothers new students, disproved before birth by someone who outranks them in their own branch, are telling the world we should not be alarmed. The lesson here is that information, intelligence and rank mean nothing. Big cheese needs money to feed the lie.

This isn't the worst news yet though. The worst is that DU gets hotter and more radioactive. More deadly. The half-life of depleted uranium is 4.5 billion years, the age of the earth. The uranium 238, when it decays turns into more radioactive isotopes that are more radioactive by millions and billions of times. So, slowly over time, the areas that have been bombed will become more and more radioactive. This is not conspiracy theory, this is Scientists with PhD's quantitatively saying that it is not appropriate for my mothers new students to continue making ignorant decisions about the state of our existence.

"What are the impacts of this though Dennis? How can we tell anything really happened? It is radioactive, microwave, nuclear, but I can't see anything, I can't tell anything different."

In October of 2003 I reported to the World Uranium weapons conference in Hamburg, Germany that the United States had been training the troops to respond to nuclear attacks for decades.

Bodies in the impact zone, (back cover photo) of the weaponry were melted. That is the hell the troops see. Not since the flame thrower has anything so inhumane been used. American troops were exposed to the left over, alpha and gamma radiation from the bombing raids. The civilians who traveled the land after battle had ended were carrying, eating, and drinking these alpha particles and were exposed to any gamma radiation occurring.

Many medical doctors have verified adverse health effects from personal experience.
Listed affects:
Reactive airway disease, neurological abnormalities, kidney stones and chronic kidney pain, rashes, vision degradation and night vision losses, gum tissue problems, lymphoma, various forms of skin and organ cancer, neuro-psychological disorders, uranium in semen, sexual dysfunction, and birth defects in offspring.

Women whose husbands came back from the

Gulf War have complained that after intercourse they experience burning in their vaginal area and lose sensation. Soldier's semen has depleted uranium and chemicals flowing as hot as hell. In a study of 251 Gulf War veterans in the state of Mississippi, which was conducted by the Veterans Administration, The veterans who had birthed healthy children before they went off to the Gulf War came back, and of the children conceived and born after the Gulf War, 67% had children with severe illnesses and deformities. These children were born without brains, without organs, without hands, without legs, with the hands attached to the shoulders. Miscarriages, who knows how many miscarriages from this event. Excuse me, but this weaponry is fucking with the gene pool.

In addition to Northern California, serious adverse health effects have been documented in employees and residents living near Puducah, Kentucky; Portsmouth, Ohio; Los Alamos, New Mexico; Oak Ridge, Tennessee and Hanford, Washington. Additionally employees at uranium manufacturing or processing facilities in New York, Tennessee, and the four corners area of southwest Colorado have repeatedly reported adverse health effects similar to those reported by verified Gulf War DU casualties.

In the courts of international law, under the Geneva conventions and all other treaties, depleted uranium is illegal. The United Nations has banned it! It is as if Americans are the last ones to know. It is illegal, America is breaking the fucking law. If life doesn't matter, and truth doesn't matter, if science doesn't matter (quantitatively nor qualitatively), and the law doesn't matter, what matters? Please, somebody tell those soldiers that they are fighting for their lives with science and the law on their side. It is not fair to go into battle any other way.

"Please, somebody Support the Truth."

Again, everybody together.

"Yes, Drill Sergeant."